# How the Elephant Got Its Trunk

Jane Langford
Illustrated by Mike Terry

Long ago, all the elephants in Africa had short noses. Today, all the elephants in Africa have long trunks.

Why do they have long trunks? They have long trunks because of one little elephant.

Little Elephant liked to ask questions. He asked, "Where?" and "What?" and "When?" But the question Little Elephant liked to ask most often was "Why?"

Little Elephant often watched the other animals. He watched them and then asked them questions. One day, Little Elephant went to the river to watch Turtle. "Turtle, why do you have a shell?" he asked.

"How would I know?" said Turtle. "Stop asking so many questions!"

Little Elephant went to watch Lion. "Lion, why do you have a curly mane?" he asked.

"What a question!" said Lion. "I don't know."

Little Elephant went to watch Chimp. "Chimp, why do you have long arms?" he asked.

"I don't know," said Chimp. "Stop asking so many questions."

"This is no good. I want answers!" cried Little
Elephant. "Who can answer my questions?"
"I can! I can!" said Kolo Kolo Bird.

So Little Elephant asked Kolo Kolo Bird lots of questions. He asked, "Where?" and "What?" and "When?" Kolo Kolo Bird answered all Little Elephant's questions.

"I have one more question and then I will stop," said Little Elephant. "What does Crocodile eat for dinner?"

"Oh, my! What does Crocodile eat for dinner?" said Kolo Kolo Bird. "What a question! Why don't you go down to the river and ask him!"

"Yes, I will. I will go down to the river and ask Crocodile. Thank you, Kolo Kolo Bird, thank you!" said Little Elephant.

Little Elephant went down to the river.
"Crocodile! Crocodile! What do you eat for
dinner?" he asked.

Crocodile smiled. "Bend down, and I will tell you!" he said.

So Little Elephant bent down.
"I often eat turtles for dinner," said
Crocodile. "But today, I'm going to eat YOU!"

Little Elephant stepped back. But Crocodile was too fast. He snapped his jaws around Little Elephant's nose. **SNAP**!

"Let go!" shouted Little Elephant. But Crocodile would not let go. "Help!" shouted Little Elephant. "Help me!"

Snake heard Little Elephant calling. He came
as fast as he could. "I'm coming, Little Elephant!"
Snake cried. "I'm coming!"

Snake wrapped his tail around a tree. Then he wrapped himself around Little Elephant. "Now pull!" Snake called to Little Elephant. "Pull hard!"

Little Elephant pulled and Snake pulled too.
But Crocodile would not let go! Little Elephant's
nose grew longer and longer!

"Pull harder!" shouted Snake. "Pull harder!"

All at once, Crocodile let go. He fell back into the water. **SPLASH!**

"I've got you! I've got you!" Snake shouted to Little Elephant.

Little Elephant sat down under the tree and cried. His short nose had been pulled so hard that it was now very, very long!

"Oh, no!" cried Little Elephant. "What am I going to do? My nose is too long. I look silly!"

"Now, now, Little Elephant. You don't look silly at all," said Snake.

"But what can I do with a nose like this?" cried
Little Elephant. He wiped away a tear with his
new, long trunk.

"You can do that!" cried Snake.

"But how will I eat with a nose like this?" cried Little Elephant. He pulled up some grass with his new, long trunk and put it in his mouth.

"Like that!" cried Snake.

"But how am I going to drink?" cried Little Elephant. He put his new, long trunk into the river and got some water.

"Just like that!" cried Snake.

Little Elephant smiled. "I like this long nose more than the short one," he said. "I will go and show it to my family. No other animal in Africa has a nose like this!"

Little Elephant's family asked lots of questions about his new, long nose. They asked, "Where?" and "What?" and "When?" But none of them asked "Why?" They could all see why!